Kiva

a chapbook

David Appelbaum

ISBN: 978-81-19654-72-7

First Edition: 2024
Rs. 200/-

Cyberwit.net
HIG 45 Kaushambi Kunj, Kalindipuram
Allahabad - 211011 (U.P.) India
http://www.cyberwit.net
Tel: +(91) 9415091004
E-mail: info@cyberwit.net

Printed at Repro India Limited.

Dedication

To Amiya Chakravarty

songs that were only a song still to come.

Maurice Blanchot

Contents

Graph

a double slope
redounds

in tendrils
of the heart

sports downy spikes
that weigh mood

freight hope
with bitter-sweet
complicity

it's a full moon
a new season

it's beautiful
when one thing

changes to another
while staying the same

to mock
eternity

At the center

the labyrinth
on a window screen

is spider-art
flourished since
the late Pleistocene

gestures toward
here and there
at he same time future

a beastly brain
can't be hungry

a black hole
for fly or ant

no gold thread
to unwrite

the mommy myth
in plea for justice

no bully waits
at the center

Melodies

songs in my brain
without mention

address imagined
kisses to you

dry, feckless ooo's
light as oxygen

phantasmic whats-its-name
perfume my body

moist skeins of pores

is it plausible
that mute clichés

like monkey chatter

can eviscerate sorrow?

Pleasure principle

they've gone flit
the stomata

on their job, pressing
atom from atom

like a French
coffee maker

delivering ambrosia
across a gap

between life
and living

(do I have it backwards?)

exhale, inhale, mimic

their squawks and jerks
in love,

as if to say
to placid fronds

'play it please again'

Speech

the idea there's this
next to say

persists on air-cushioned
fuzz from catkins

that brush my lips
an inspired caress

that emboldens a feel
of insertion

rejoinder or repartee

but all that comes
is 'Mmmm, mmm!'

how words meet
a dead end

elogquent.

Vision

mesh is
sunlight that doesn't come
clean

though it's where it does
that we see it

the point at which
insistence becomes
surprising

as, for instance, why
the night sky

isn't bright glare
with stars in the trillions

all God's messages
as 'it'

so to say, letters
chart a testing
for eyesight

that's too dim to see

Kintsugi

what's broke
can't be new again

like a promise
or a thing called heart

grifting says
otherwise

ragged edges
swabbed together

pasted, taped
bound, retied

with glue of compassion
that art uses

makes whole
to different ends—

because life won't,
or won't quite

make new
with alteration.

Danger

a nest behind the stop sign
with three bullet holes

three Cyclops look back
one yellow eye, two green

sparrows dart
oblivious as sheep of scripts

current politics
past sins

cameras are mounted
on walls, in trees

I'd like to tell them
they're under surveillance

alive onscreen
I'd like to remind them

it's no big thing
no blame

when youthful
disaffection

starts the war
it will end

with no casualty.

Eye sore

I'm not,
but an eye-person

would be nutso not to see
pine trees
the size of a finger

now-crushed tips
nail a fragrance
as ditzy as basil

knuckles of existence
dissolved to breath
as I kneel replanting

out of nowhere
a fly strikes me
right between the eyes

where vision
succumbs to folly

the oldest joke
on earth

To the brim

that part of a head
under a hat

is barely real since
it's barely there

not private exactly
without being public

shaded but heated

my mind is like
the edge of the brim too

lopsided, rakish
irregular

as the owner
of the hat

I walk home
thinking it mine

though it clearly fit
a head

two sizes large

Dirigible

the Fuji blimp patrols
a giddy frizz

of skyline
recognizable
in order to be

aerially comforting
an infant
swaddled in a stroller

as if a flying object
could be

image of the mother—

love settled fitfully
on the ad line

as a butterfly
its nectar

Facts

mud-swaddled arrowroot
a colony
up and down

banks of . . . .

innocent endless
iterations

(the devil loves
the word)

as if survival
were in question

beside acid-
eaten rocks

as if 'more' draws
a lightning flash

as life lives
in that arc:

facticity

Delivery

brown sea mist
corner
of a Rembrandt

limits
what is known

heavy-lidded
fatum
streaming pure

self-love

unusually banal
in day dawning
cherry pink
blossoms

on a windshield
unrolling news

flung on front lawns
by the errand boy

tells the city
nothing
more important

than the scent

Chrysalis

a butterfly lights
on an oil stain
wings beat, beating . . .

the brain causes
things to blink
a half-second after

there is rest
there is motion

in between there is
an air
of importance

nothing other than
a lump
in the throat:

it matters

Riddle

the gray-green catkin
apostrophizes
atop a dead pigeon

'whenever two are gathered'
. . . .

by which act is
the name charged

tongue-in-cheek breviary
so to keep

the body unspoiled
from grammatically

inert matter
divine lips

still await
an untouchable kiss

of sensation

Sideline

sawdust under
oblique rust

rides a city sign

begin again

sawdust drooling
a phlegmy rust

blotches a city sign

then twists round
the letter 'o'

to highlight
a loose, wanton

substrate, knotweed
as it curls

by the gravely side
of the tracks

what the mineral
mass of memory

adds or deletes—
the crime?

Clandestiny

up the stairs
it's gravity

bug spray
gaiters
'A Man in Moscow'

pull of
resistance

in order to
neutralize

family photos
plaid slippers

carpet brooms
world globes

from third grade
geography

did you bury
the matter

in lists
in order to

leave it downstairs?

Sum

morning sun
speckles my window
and is brightened

eye spots that fleck
splotch or mottle

so many metonyms
for a bit
of *schmutz*

grandstanding
grabs the spotlight

gnats grimace
at human
purpose

instead, breathe
third force
to let happen

a sugar rush

Venus at Willendorf

chunk of slag
hips, an ancient goddess

proof scoria alone
is fertile enough

to people thoughts
of rebirth—

what isn't someone
else's metaphor

for living a life
unhad

never prayed for
never dreampt

really felt?

Street scene

strewn
like bijoux
over tarmac

aspen lobes
downy, pendulous
throaty

surrender
their wanton ways

their only lives
wait
for no end

such inflorescence
now attends

the sound
of the second coming—

the street cleaner
metal brush

Hellsgate

catkins
down at the mouth

dangle fruit
over Tantalus

in a whirligig
of affection

their instance—
hunger's—

limits what's known

self-love, I,
interrupted

his fingers
bud-nipped

grip

the bland seed
of purgatory

On the beach

the smaller serves
the larger
a figure of speech

like
kick heels
might
a state of sheer bliss

or A for Big Apple
that reenacts that bite

of sin in the city

it's secret branding
a hopeful tag

the skimpy red bikini
reads 'synecdoche'

which you think,
French for cleaning
instructions

Party

pink flamingo
birthday pant suit

'vibrant,' 'overdrawn'
'illogical'

traipsed the day through
carelessly, lewdly
bouncing off walls

unwilling to coexist
with a juggernaut

of the present

sensing us with its
singular
way of coming across

like the 'as' in come
as you are

reticence

go figure

Romance

high-flying propagator

woodbine with rare
erotics

snapped to attention
in the last freeze

her short phrases
insufficient

to give voice to
the neutron sheen

crispating buds
slithery tendril

it reminds us
music makes strange

bedfellows
a hairy stalk

rubs against a cedar
post

love worn thin

Constitutional

flat out
there are things you'll
be asked to note

absence of green
on the dusky forest floor
for one

how it effaces
evening
prune-lipped, high-heeled

hidden in vine leaves
thin, with pink fringes
of future inebriants

round eyes, protrude
brittle brown stalks
see to the scripts

we read, producing
petrified relics:
our evening stroll

Quick one

hot take:
the wind
has wound
the rope
tighter

the bottle's
neck
stiff, upright

seemed to hear
more acute
than belief

what is not
yet quite
itself
dissolve

into
titters,
mistook
identity

Burning the tree

word had it
the squat spruce

once a Christmas tree

shivered under
the north dock

to put winter to rest
surrendering

its feckless
life in ruin

needles
loosened, fell

in brown piles of dung

if only to avoid

burning
at the stake

a heretical
martyr

Giveaway

a white shirt
left on the clothesline
snuggles around
a windy corner
in starched egoism

embarrassed by
its lack of skin
that leaves wiggle room
to maneuver

oblated it forms
syllables
mantras really
that make no sense

when our eyelids
lie flat, when
we are 'listening
stations'

its love scenes
wear collars thin—
a seedy cloth

once put out
to sunshine
and left for
puffy chests to bear

At the spa

golden toned
belly

abs
entia

the thrill
we get out of

our own self-
loathing

incites us
to know

our private
moves

in all moments
granting

war
with friction

It listeth

wind in trellis
raises the rosebush
to new heights

in spots attachment
tangles brambles

is it pleased with itself
as self-reference
professes

red hips protrude
on weak stems

or it is asking to shout
Yiddish
like an angry old man

who produces
scripts reading

current goings-on,
this, for one?

Hedges

'it's a doozy'

between the crotch
of the oak tree

the sun rises
with white lies

its journals sway
the finale

. . .

that virtue swaddles its own
reward

disproves the benefits
system

. . .

making things up
is another way

of taking things
down

the way the bird
preaches

without saying

DST

time squirms
to get over the hill
clocks are phased
back and out

to flip the script
(yammer nonsense)

people count on
being wrong about

sensations of lateness

I am disagreeably
awake

my head is thick
with the right day

what time is it?

Glare

it's all disappearing

secreted light
floats a locked gaze

photons stuck
on a sticky thought

your eyes
a void dead center

that makes this spider
a strange attractor

and you, cancelled,
a stain

in the first person
told by

neither wave nor thing

but whiteness
of the whale

Start over

I wrote nothing on the wall
traipsing through careless
verbs

like oolong or funnel or glaze

sending ripples over what
you'd say you read

start over

I wrote no thing, which is not
nothing
lolling with a dog's tongue

on command from a poster
in obedience school

drooling into an abyss
so that the last gee

touches the new (!) Milkbone
where it would enter
the socket

male to female

Timetable

the multi-personality disorder
of many people who wait
for the late bus
mulls different times

daylight savings, Greenwich mean
Siberian standard

no one on present time
confusion can produce

a transfiguration, single
to plural, each echoes 'Aha'

to themselves
voice chases voice
around a squat kiosk

a lump in the throat
for sorrow
a suck on a pebble
for faith

try whimpering

'I'm who I am'

Landscape

a miniature house
green roof
on a lace doily

some froufrou fronds
on top
catch early sun

each joist says
'cover me'
then 'I'm desperate'

someone will weld
under the portico
(with careful laughter)

trying to nail it
to conjure up
the human condition

as a parody
a journey refused
with a lesson

the *mot juste* will
sound a lot like

brouhaha

Space

illegible graph—
the sky

day-lit but with stars

watch yourself
gasp

while scattered around
your feet

the fossiled remains
a planet's life

now under camera—
eye of Mars Rover

what novelty has
promised:

eternity's gaze
on playthings of time

same old dust
same old stones

www.ingramcontent.com/pod-product-compliance
Lightning Source LLC
Chambersburg PA
CBHW022203160726
48282CB00024B/317
* 9 7 8 8 1 1 9 6 5 4 7 2 7 *